MW01470533

you are
more

you are
more

carmen rasmusen herbert

DESERET
BOOK

Salt Lake City, Utah

Library of Congress Cataloging-in-Publication Data
Herbert, Carmen Rasmusen, author.
  You are more / Carmen Rasmusen Herbert.
      pages cm
  Includes bibliographical references.
  ISBN 978-1-60907-713-6 (hardbound : alk. paper)
1. Herbert, Carmen Rasmusen. 2. Country musicians—Biography.
3. Singers—Biography. I. Title.
  ML420.H3753A3 2013
  782.421642092—dc23
  [B]   2013023817

Printed in the United States of America
R. R. Donnelley, Crawfordsville, IN

10 9 8 7 6 5 4 3 2 1

For my mom, who always believed I could be more.

And for my boys, Boston, Beckham, and Briggs,
who've made me so.

Who are you?

What do you want to become?

When I was growing up, I knew exactly what I wanted to be when I got older. There was never any question in my mind: I wanted to be a country singer. And I wanted to be a mother.

In the fourth grade we had a career day at school. We were all asked to write down three possible life professions. I wrote down only one, of course: country singer.

We were actually told not to put things like

"basketball player" or "dancer" or "singer" because, well, odds were that we would probably end up doing "normal" things like teaching, doctoring, or lawyering.

Not me. I just knew I would achieve my goals someday. I always had an extreme amount of confidence and truly, honestly believed that I could do and be whatever I wanted.

My parents also believed I could do anything. (In fact, they were probably the ones who put the idea into my head in the first place!) My sweet mother signed me up to sing at every county fair, every ward party, and every talent show in Utah (or so it seemed). I participated in singing and music groups from the age of five. I was in private singing lessons from the age of ten. I also took piano and guitar lessons.

I was doing everything "right" to try to make it big.

When I was about fourteen, my mom came into my room late one night. She sat at the foot of my bed with a big smile on her face and said she had something very special to tell me that my vocal coach, Dean Kaelin, had told her.

"I don't want you to go sharing this with a lot of people," she said. "Keep this hidden in your heart, like a little jewel you wouldn't want anyone to steal."

She then told me that my teacher had expressed his confidence in me as well. "Carmen has the potential to go all the way," he had said.

"Really?" I asked. I was elated. I couldn't believe that my vocal coach, who had worked with hundreds of students over many years, had told my mom that HE believed in ME. She wanted me to know what he'd said so that if I ever started to doubt myself, I could remember it. She wanted me to believe I could do whatever I set my mind to do.

"You can," she said.

I had faith in myself, but that faith was even stronger because someone believed in me.

What if someone told you that they knew you had the potential to go all the way—that they believed in YOU? Would you have confidence pursuing your goals and dreams?

There is One who has had many years of experience. He has helped thousands reach their goals. He knows you better than anyone, and He believes in you. He knows you have the potential to go all the way.

So much more precious than the little jewel of confidence my singing coach gave me is the absolute vote of confidence my Heavenly Father gives me.

We can trust our Heavenly Father. He knows us. He knows our potential. He believes in us! We can believe the Lord when He says, "With God all things are possible" (Matthew 19:26).

If He believes in me, I can believe in me too.

What if we all lived with that kind of unwavering faith? What if, no matter what anyone said or did, we knew exactly WHO we were and WHAT we were doing and WHERE we were going? We would live our lives like we had nothing to lose.

In fact, we're taught that if we build our

foundation upon the rock of Christ, it will be "a sure foundation, a foundation whereon if men build they cannot fall" (Helaman 5:12).

One afternoon in early October 2002, when I was home from school because of a badly sprained ankle, I received a phone call from my dad. He said, "How would you like to try out for *American Idol?*"

I was shocked and completely intrigued. "Um, sure, I'd probably love to. When? Where?"

"Today," my dad said.

It was three P.M. I had to video record myself singing a song a capella and get it out to FOX 13 News studios by five. I didn't think it was possible. For just a second, I didn't want to try. It probably wasn't worth the hassle. I was still in my pajamas. I hadn't done my hair. We didn't own a video camera!

As I was going through all this in my mind, I heard my dad say: "What have you got to lose?"

Those six words changed my life.

Through a rather unbelievable series of fortunate events, I got to participate in the Salt Lake tryouts for *Idol*. Through each stage, my mom would say, "Now if you only make callbacks, that's okay. No matter what, this is a good experience!" I remember reading through the contract and rules on my parents' bed after I tried out. The words *One will be chosen as the "Salt Lake Idol"* popped out at me, and I wanted more than anything for that "one" to be me.

A week later, I found out I was chosen.

I'll never forget the day I drove with my mom to the airport to fly out to L.A. to audition for *American Idol*. I was thinking, "My dreams are coming true. This is the most unbelievable thing." It felt amazing. As we drove, my mom had a huge smile on her face.

"You were meant to do this," she kept saying.

I feel so incredibly lucky and blessed to have the mother I have. She has always been my biggest fan. What if, in everything we did, we had someone cheering us on, saying, "You can do this!" Wouldn't we be more confident?

Well, guess what? You ARE meant to do this. You ARE meant to be here. You have amazing capabilities. You were given incredible talents from your Heavenly Father. He is your biggest fan. He wants you to succeed more than anyone does.

And with Him, you can.

So I flew out to Hollywood to audition for the infamous Simon Cowell. Everything was magical about that trip. I stayed on a street called Carmen Ave. My room number was 207 (seven is my lucky number). I had my nails fixed by a woman who claimed to have done Paula Abdul's.

The night before I auditioned, I went out to eat with my mom. I got up to use the restroom and started humming while waiting in line outside the door. A waiter walked by and told me I had a pretty voice.

Later, he asked me what I was there for. I told him I was auditioning for *Idol.* He said, "I have a feeling about you . . . you're going to make it." What? A totally random stranger said he had a "feeling" that I was going to make it? It was so weird! My mom, of course, looked at me and said, "See? You're meant to do this!"

Turns out, the waiter was right. I made it through two auditions before singing for the dreaded judges, Simon and Paula. (Randy was out shooting a Krispy Kreme commercial that day.)

After making it through to Hollywood, I was cut the day before they picked the top thirty-two contestants. *Devastated* wouldn't even begin to describe what I was feeling. I felt totally and completely let down. Every time I went to sleep, I hoped I would wake up and realize I was just dreaming.

What about all those "feelings" everyone had? Why was my mom so sure I would make it? I felt silly for believing.

Has that ever happened to you? You trust in the Spirit, you follow a prompting, and things don't work out the way you expected them to. We can't always see God's plan for us. Sometimes, even when we think we're so sure of something, it doesn't fall into place like we imagine it will.

The point is to
not give up.
Keep
trusting.
Keep
going.

"Only at our peril would we allow doubt or devils to sway us from [God's true] path. Hope on. Journey on. Honestly acknowledge your questions and your concerns, but first and forever fan the flame of your faith, because all things are possible to them that believe" (Jeffrey R. Holland, "'Lord, I Believe,'" *Ensign,* May 2013, 95).

For some reason, even months later, I still believed.

One warm afternoon in February, I received a phone call from the producers of *American Idol* to come back and try out for the "wild card" show. It was then that I was chosen by Simon Cowell to be in the top twelve.

I can still hear my dad's enthusiastic shout of "No way!" when I told him over the phone that I had made it.

I was so unbelievably excited to be on the show. I knew I would probably be tested vocally, emotionally, and mentally. But I didn't know how much my faith and standards would be tested.

The familiar question of "Who are you?" was thrown at us almost daily. "Who do you want to look like?" we were asked. "Who do you want to sound like? Who do you want to dress like?"

Who are you?

I was the only member of The Church of Jesus Christ of Latter-day Saints on the show, and pretty soon, word got around that I was a Mormon.

And then the questions really started.

"Who, exactly, are Mormons?"

Well, my seminary teacher must have been inspired, because a few weeks into the show, a huge box arrived for me from him. I opened it up, and inside, filling the box to the brim, were *For the Strength of Youth* pamphlets and pass-along cards. So, I handed them out to people. When contestants started asking me tough questions, I would say, "Well, if you turn to page five of the *For the Strength of Youth* pamphlet, you will read . . ."

I was able to share my testimony and a little of what I believed with them. And when I did, something amazing happened. Instead of making fun of me or saying I was silly for believing the way I did, my fellow contestants went overboard to try to protect me. They kept saying they didn't want to "corrupt" Carmen. They wanted to keep me clean and pure. Isn't that interesting? They could see that I was different, and they wanted me to stay that way. So I not only had a lot of pressure from family and friends back home to stay true to who I was, but now my new friends and competitors were watching me too.

One night we decided to watch a movie. We had dinner waiting for us upstairs, and I was the last one to dish up my food. I walked downstairs, sat down, and was just getting ready to take a big bite when Rickey Smith, one of my good friends, leaned over and said, "Carmen, baby . . . this movie's rated R."

My heart sank. I was sad not only because they had chosen an R-rated show to watch but because I wouldn't get that time to spend with my friends. I knew that if I walked upstairs, I'd be the only one.

I picked up my plate and stood to leave. All of a sudden, Kim Cauldwell, another good friend, piped up, "Rickey! She's eighteen and her mom's not here. She can stay and watch it." I think she thought she was sticking up for me.

Rickey then said, "But she's a Mormon, and she said Mormons don't watch rated-R movies!" Rickey remembered me reading him the page in the *FTSOY* pamphlet that says, "Do not attend, view, or participate in anything that is vulgar, immoral, violent, or pornographic in any way. . . . Have the courage to walk out of a movie . . . if what you see or hear drives away the Spirit." If I had stayed, what would be his view of the type of person I was? Perhaps his opinion of Mormons would have changed. I was maybe the only Mormon he knew, and if I had stayed and watched that movie, he might have thought that Mormons say one thing but do another, that they don't really practice what they preach. I knew I had to stick to my standards and set an example for these people, some of whom were learning about the Church for the first time.

I went upstairs and called my mom. I cried. It was hard being alone! I'm not going to tell you it's always going to be easy to live the standards of the Church. It isn't.

But is it always worth it? ABSOLUTELY! I want to share a truth with you that has helped me make good choices in difficult situations. It is this: YOU WILL NEVER REGRET MAKING A RIGHT DECISION. No matter how hard it is. No matter if you're the only one making that decision. No matter if your friends make fun of you for wearing that modest swimming suit, or for choosing to not go to prom two days before you turn sixteen (like my older

You will
NEVER
regret
living the way
you *know* you
should live.

sister did), or for staying home on the weekend instead of going to a party you know might be bad.

I also learned that night that I wasn't really alone. When we make right choices, we have the Holy Ghost to be our CONSTANT companion (see Doctrine and Covenants 121:46). Not our sometimes companion. Not an every-now-and-then companion. Our constant companion. But of course, it's up to us.

One of my favorite scriptures is Doctrine and Covenants 68:6, which reads, "Wherefore, be of good cheer, and do not fear, for I the Lord am with you, and will stand by you."

Who can we have standing by us who would be greater than the Lord? I truly felt strength beyond my own helping me to make righteous choices. Sometimes my mom said she would be cooking in the kitchen when she'd get a feeling that I needed her. She said she would drop everything right then and there and pray for me. My little brother or sister would come bounding in, and she would have disappeared suddenly. "Mom?" they would call, and she would pop up, having been on her knees behind our kitchen island, praying for me. I felt those prayers.

Something she prayed for a lot was that I would have the strength to protect my virtue and keep my body and actions modest.

A lot of people try to define themselves by their look. How we did our hair, how we did our makeup, what we were going to wear—we were being defined by our style constantly on *American Idol.* And style, it was whispered, was the most important thing in Hollywood.

A lot has changed in the ten years since I was on *Idol.* We sang karaoke instead of with a live band. We didn't win cars, that's for sure! We didn't have famous guest coaches.

We also were responsible for picking out—and paying for—our own outfits.

The first time I went shopping with the stylists, it was right after I made the wild card show.

My mom was with me, as I was only seventeen and needed a parent or guardian with me at all times. We went out shopping with the rest of the contestants. I hadn't really told anyone yet about my standards, and so when the stylists started pulling things for me to try on that were, say, a little on the skimpy side, I got kind of nervous about what to say.

They'd hold up a tank top, and I'd shake my head, saying I didn't like the color. They'd get a skintight, low-cut dress, and I'd say the material wasn't quite right. They'd bring out a pair of short shorts, and I'd say I didn't like the cut. And on and on.

Finally, seeing as I was one of the last ones to pick out an outfit, they said, "Okay. What do you LIKE?"

"Well, I don't really feel comfortable showing my shoulders," I said.

"Oh. Okay," they said.

"Or my stomach," I quickly added. "Or too much leg. Or back. Or front. Can't be too tight. Or revealing."

Their eyes got bigger as my list got longer. I was so worried that these professionals would be frustrated or think my values were seriously outdated, especially for modern Hollywood. But they were actually very supportive. In fact, one day as I was out looking for a top, I came out of the dressing room in a cute, frilly, cap-sleeved shirt, and the stylist took one look at me and said, "Oh no, I think that shows too much shoulder," and found something else for me to try.

One day, around the fifth week of *Idol*, I went out only a day or two before our show looking for an outfit to wear. I found a silky, pretty, tie-dyed dress that was cinched at the top. It was a tube-top, so I planned on wearing my dressy denim jacket over the top of it. Because rehearsals were so grueling that week and it was so difficult to go out shopping, I picked everything out last minute. The shoes were even brought to my room late the night before the show.

The day of the show came, and as I walked into

the dressing room to change into my outfit, I noticed that my jacket looked a little too big for the dress. I had neglected to try everything on the night before, just hoping and praying everything would turn out all right.

Well, it didn't look so good. I came walking out, and the stylists immediately panicked.

"Why didn't you see if this would work last night?" they asked, frantically trying to find me something else to wear. I had no excuse except an exhausted brain that wasn't quite functioning at an optimal level.

"I'm sorry," was all I managed to get out.

"Well," they said, "you're just going to have to wear the dress without the jacket."

I then remembered a black T-shirt that I was planning on wearing for a taped interview with Ryan Seacrest after the live show. I ran back to the dressing room, slipped it on under the gown, and came back out.

"No," they said. "We don't like the T-shirt, either."

Truth be told, neither did I.

But I knew I had no other choice. I WAS NOT going to compromise my modesty. Now, some might think, "Come on! It's not that big of a deal." But I knew I couldn't let my family down. I couldn't let my Heavenly Father down—not when He'd blessed me so much and I firmly believed it was because of Him I had made it that far in the first place.

My parents were watching. My siblings were watching. My friends were watching. My ward was watching.

The world was watching.

Who was I going to be?

That night, I walked out on to the stage to sing Billy Joel's "And So It Goes." Some of my friends had driven out to see me and were seated in the audience. As soon as I walked onstage, I saw their eyes grow big and their mouths drop. I kind of looked ridiculous. I was mortified, and it showed. I got bad reviews from the judges. It was probably my worst performance.

BUT. *I did not regret making a right decision!* Later, I was able to auction that hideous dress off for charity. It made quite the impression back home, but for me, the lesson it taught me lasted a lifetime. No matter what—modesty is worth it.

I firmly believe that God loves His daughters SO MUCH, and He wants us to dress modestly because He wants us to save and protect our most sacred, beautiful bodies. I'm not going to pretend I was always perfect in this area. I made mistakes and learned, just like anyone else. But being in the spotlight really opened my eyes as to why modesty is more important than ever.

It's so easy to sell out. It's easy to get attention for your body. But what do I really want to be remembered for? Do I want to be known for my body or for my spirit and mind? Do I want people to talk about how skinny, sexy, or stunning I am, or how sweet, spiritual, and strong I am?

Do I want people looking AT my body or IN my eyes?

One day my mom received a phone call from a friend. She said, "When Carmen walks out on that stage, it's like there's a light that turns on." Did you know that many people can actually SEE a physical difference when they look at a member of The Church of Jesus Christ of Latter-day Saints who is living the standards? That light is the light of Christ.

"Verily, verily, I say unto you, I give unto you to be the light of this people. . . . Therefore let your light so shine before this people, that they may see your good works and glorify your Father who is in heaven" (3 Nephi 12:14, 16).

Heavenly Father provided ways for me to keep that light, even when things seemed impossible.

People magazine did an entire issue based on our season of *American Idol*. The contestants were in several group shots together, and then each of us was to have a one-page spotlight in the magazine.

We showed up at a gorgeous hotel to get our

pictures taken, and there we learned that we were each going to be given a "theme." For example, one of the contestants had a "forest" theme and was photographed among gorgeous trees, flowers, and greenery. Another had a "music" theme and was pictured in front of an old-fashioned sound board in a recording studio. Another was in a bathroom, for some reason, and was seated next to the tub and toilet. We all kind of felt sorry for that person!

My theme was "old Hollywood," and I was told that a classic white Mustang was waiting for me out on the streets of L.A., with spotlights shining all around.

I waited in the beautiful, extravagant hotel room suite for the stylist to come give me my outfit and take me up to hair and makeup.

"Okay!" he said, breezing in. "Here's your outfit. I have this . . . *vision* . . . of you looking like Britney Spears, sprawled across the seats of the car. It will be fantastic. YOU will be fantastic! Here's what you'll be wearing. I wanted you in pink and white," he declared.

A tiny halter top and miniskirt were handed over to me. Nervously, I looked at my mom, who was there with me. She raised her eyebrows but didn't say anything. She wanted me to make my own choice.

"Um, I'm sorry," I said to the stylist, "but I can't wear that."

"Excuse me?" he said.

"I'm a good little Mormon girl!" I said with a smile, hoping he would smile back.

"I'll be right back," he said, and he left.

I sat down next to my mom with a pit in my stomach. What was I going to do? I turned to my mom for help.

"While you were talking, I noticed a shirt hanging in that closet over there," my mom said, pointing. "What if you asked the stylist if you could wear that instead?" Hanging in the closet of the next hotel suite was a red, long-sleeved, button-up shirt. It was very country-looking and had beautiful jewels sparkling all over it.

"Mom," I said, shaking my head, "I can't just waltz into someone's closet and steal a random shirt! I don't even know who it belongs to. Besides, what would I wear with it?"

"The jeans you have on look fine," my mom said, apparently disregarding the wrinkles and token food stain that's on every pair of jeans I own.

Meanwhile, the stylist came back in and took my hand. "I want to speak with you alone," he said, shooting my mom a "look."

"Now," he said, closing the door, "you need to trust me. I know what looks good. Do you know who I am?" I actually didn't at the time, but I nodded anyway to be polite.

"I have this vision . . ." he started again, and I quickly interrupted.

"What if I wore this?" I asked, pointing to the shirt we were conveniently standing by.

He took the shirt off the hanger and said, "This

looks like a $500 shirt. I don't know whose it is. It must have been left over from another shoot."

"Mind if I try it on?" I asked. I think at this point he was so exhausted with me arguing with him that he agreed.

I quickly put the shirt on and came out to show it to him.

He stopped, looked me up and down, and said, "That actually looks really good. Okay, you can wear it. Let's go."

Two weeks later, the magazines were shipped to us. Clay Aiken ripped the box open and we all started flipping through.

"Look at you, Miss Centerfold," Clay said to me. "What did you tell the editors?"

"What?" I had no idea what he was talking about.

"Oh, jeez," Clay said, rolling his eyes as I flipped through the magazine frantically. "You must have said something."

Quickly I turned to my page . . . and was very surprised.

"Out of all us twelve contestants," he said, "you were the only one who got a TWO-page spread."

I couldn't believe it. I thought that if anything, maybe they had been upset with how difficult I was and had Photoshopped a mustache on my face or something!

At the bottom of my page, it read:

"Well Covered: A Mormon, Rasmusen says she isn't comfortable wearing low-cut or overly sexy stage costumes. 'If I become the American Idol,' says the singer, 'I can prove you don't have to sell your body to sell your songs.'" The next page talked about how my stylist and I had disagreed on my look.

I laughed at this. I thought it was hilarious that they thought it was such a big deal that they just had to say something in print.

As much as *People* would perhaps try to convince the world otherwise, I actually did love getting "makeovers," as long as they were up to my—or rather the Lord's—standards. I may have been more restrictive than the other contestants as to what clothing I could wear, but makeup and hair-wise, there was a lot more wiggle room.

I spent many hours—hours and hours and hours—in hair and makeup chairs. We had the very best professionals in the business "working" on us to make us look like perfect Barbie dolls onstage. We were airbrushed. We were painted. We were plucked, shaved, primped, fluffed, sprayed, glossed, brushed, and smoothed.

We were made to look "perfect."

And we were touched up during every commercial break so as not to prove otherwise.

It was all very mind-twisting, to tell you the truth. On the one hand, I loved having my hair and makeup done. But since then, I've thought, "What's so wrong about the way I look naturally that I have to have so much time spent making me look 'camera ready'?" I started to get so used to my "stage look" that I began to feel much less pretty on the days I wasn't all glammed up.

There is something very, very wrong with that way of thinking.

One night I was getting ready for bed. I took out my fake hair extensions and laid them on the bed. I peeled off my fake eyelashes and put them back in the box. I washed the artwork off my lids, cheeks, and lips, and scrubbed my face clean. I took off my six-inch heels, my blinged-out jewelry, and my padded bra.

Then I looked at my mom.

She was stifling a laugh.

"What?" I asked, smiling myself.

"What will it be like on your wedding night?" she asked with a grin. "Hold on a minute, hon! Let me just take off my hair . . . and my lashes . . . and wash my face. Do you recognize me now?"

I knew she was just teasing me, but she had a point: I had better not be basing my self-esteem on looks alone. That kind of "beauty" can be wiped away in an instant. What took hours to put on only takes seconds to take off.

If I based my feelings of self-worth on who I was externally, my self-esteem would plummet every time I got a new wrinkle, stretch mark, pimple, or dimple. Our bodies can change very quickly.

But our souls, our spirits, our hearts can stay beautiful forever. And when we truly believe we are beautiful for who we are, others see that physically, too. The time we spend beautifying our inner selves is much more beneficial.

Does that mean I think everyone should walk around looking unkempt, unshowered, or like they don't care?

NO. In fact, I think there's a lot of truth to the statement, "If you look good, you feel good." The danger lies in letting our bodies become either a source of depression or a point of obsession.

I have learned that if you try to live up to the world's standards of beauty, you will always be let down. You will never be pretty enough, skinny

Who I am, who I *really* am, cannot be created or wiped away with a stroke of a makeup brush or washcloth.

enough, stylish enough, or good enough. You will always be chasing after something, and it's a very slippery slope. Self-worth cannot be based on the quest for outer beauty.

I made it to the Top 6 of *American Idol* before being eliminated. The emotional roller coaster I was on had made me a little sick at heart, and to be honest, it was a ride I was glad to get off.

In July of 2004, I was asked to sing at the Stadium of Fire program at Brigham Young University, opening for Reba McEntire with other reality show finalists, including David Archuleta.

It was a blast.

As I sat down after my performance, one of the girls next to me said there was a boy in the audience who wanted to meet me. I headed back to the stands during one of Reba's songs, barely able to hear anything. There I met the family of Gary R. Herbert. Gary was running for lieutenant governor of Utah at the time, with Jon Huntsman Jr. as the candidate for governor.

Gary's youngest son, Brad, was the one who

wanted to meet me. I shook his hand, signed his program, and gave his dad my number, telling him to call me if he wanted me to sing at any of his fund-raisers.

Brad took my number from his dad, and he called me several days later.

We went out on our first date a few weeks after that. I had so much fun. I had never laughed so hard. I wasn't expecting anything to happen at all—I was waiting for a missionary. Brad said that was perfectly fine, he wasn't wanting to get into anything serious right away either. (Yeah, right!) My manager was nervous that I was dating someone, but I assured him and my parents that it was nothing serious.

A few months of "casual dating" later, I realized something: I kind of liked this boy. I kind of liked him a lot. I think my manager and family began to realize this too, but again I assured them that my career was still my number-one priority. I needed to "hit it while it was still hot," as they say.

Well, about a year later, I realized that "like" had

turned to "love." Brad was the one I wanted to be with for eternity.

But . . . I was told very emphatically that my career would be over if I got married. So we exchanged promise rings instead. I gave Brad a sterling silver band that had the words "someday for forever" engraved on the inside.

About a week later, we decided that "someday" was today. We were done waiting. Through many days and nights of fervent prayer, study, and temple attendance, I made my choice. I was going to marry Brad.

Brad proposed on September 9, 2005. We went on a hike alongside a waterfall up a nearby canyon and then ate at a fancy restaurant at the Sundance resort. Part of our beautiful dinner was an oyster appetizer, and Brad had lined one of the shells with red velvet and hidden the ring in there. He then took me outside and sang Billy Joel's "She's Got a Way" to me.

I was in heaven.

Even though I chose to get married, I still

wanted to be a singer, and my dreams appeared to be as reachable as ever. Two years after Brad and I tied the knot, I signed a record deal with Lofton Creek records out of Nashville and recorded my first full-length album, *Nothin' Like the Summer.* I went on tour on a big tour bus all over the country, hitting all the major stations (my bus later went to Christina Aguilera). I went to the CMA and ACM awards. I walked the red carpet. I heard my song on the radio. I recorded a music video with Carrie Underwood's producer.

My dreams, it seemed, were all coming true.

Around this time, I met a young girl named Taylor Swift. Her record label president was the son of my record label president. I even talked to him about signing me someday.

Taylor was starting to get a lot of attention. She and I were "on the brink." When I interviewed Taylor for a show I was creating called *Hitch a Ride,* I remember thinking she sounded very determined to do whatever it took to become a superstar. After the interview, I started to wonder . . . was I?

I was asked to take off my wedding ring while I performed. I was told that people would think I was more desirable to work with if they presumed I was single. I hated that.

On tour, I kept a journal. I was so excited that my dreams were coming true. I had always wanted to be a country singer, and now here I was. I had, in fact, "made it."

But.

Several entries later, I started to write about different things instead of where my single was on the charts or what celebrity I had just talked to in the VIP artist lounge.

I wrote about feeling somewhat unhappy on the road, and not knowing why. It seemed like I had it all. But suddenly I felt like . . . maybe there was more. I started to write about wanting to become a mother.

I even called my manager on April Fool's Day to tell him I was pregnant, nearly giving him a heart attack.

Well, the joke was on me. Two days later I found out I was expecting.

Our first son, Boston, was born on December 16, 2008. A little under two years later, our second boy, Beckham, was born close to Halloween. A little over two years after that, our third boy, Briggs, was born on Valentine's Day.

One day I was in my little apartment cleaning up oatmeal that had cemented itself under the high chair. I was in scroungy old clothes. I hadn't had time to shower that day and was feeling rather frazzled. I flipped on the TV, and there, shining in a gorgeous gown, was Miss Taylor Swift. Glittering from head to toe with expensive jewels, a smile stretching from ear to ear. Single. Holding an armful of newly acquired awards. For a split second, I looked around at where I was, barely scraping by in our teeny, tiny condo with food all over the floor, and thought: "Is this my life? Did I really give up that—for this?"

Then I thought of my little boys in the other room. I thought of their sweet giggles, cherubic faces, and bright eyes. My eyes welled up with tears, and they still do every time I think about my

Fame and
FORTUNE
do not hold a candle
to *faith*
and *family.*

children. No matter how glamorous and wonderful the world of fame seems, it does not compare to the little world my husband and I have created.

I would so much rather be holding my tiny "jewels," my most precious children, in my arms than any trophy or award. They have been and always will be my most prized possessions, my true passions, my love.

I recently found a copy of a 2003 *Salt Lake Magazine* in which I was photographed and interviewed for the cover story. Flipping through, I found the article and had to chuckle a time or two at my eighteen-year-old answers. (For example, Question: Guilty Pleasure? Answer: "I love eating ice cream and watching Mary Kate and Ashley videos. The really cheesy ones.")

But one response really surprised me. When asked, "In 20 years, what do you hope people will be saying about you?" I responded with, "I hope people will say, 'She was a good example to her kids.'"

I was pretty shocked that even back in the day

when I still had stars in my eyes, my fame having "barely rolled off the assembly line," as writer Randy Harward stated, I still had that ultimate goal of being the best mom I could. I began to see that my vision of "who I am" was so much more than the country star I had always dreamed of becoming.

We make choices every day about who we are. We are constantly able to become who we want to be. And with our Heavenly Father's help, we can recognize and work toward our full potential as future royalty.

Who am I?

I am still a singer. That will always be a big part of who I am. But I am also a wife. I am a mother. Most important, I am a daughter of my Heavenly Father who wants to LIVE like I am a daughter of my Heavenly Father.

And that's who I always want to be.